SKYDIVING

Frances Ridley

Editorial Consultant – Cliff Moon

RISING ★ STARS

nasen
NASEN House, 4/5 Amber Business Village, Amber Close,
Amington, Tamworth, Staffordshire B77 4RP

Rising Stars UK Ltd.
22 Grafton Street, London W1S 4EX
www.risingstars-uk.com

Every effort has been made to trace copyright holders and
obtain their permission for use of copyright material. The
publisher will gladly receive information enabling them to
rectify any error or omission in subsequent editions.
All facts are correct at time of going to press.

Text © Rising Stars UK Ltd.
The right of Frances Ridley to be identified as the author
of this work has been asserted by her in accordance with
the Copyright, Design and Patents Act, 1988.

Published 2006
Reprinted 2006, 2008

Cover design: Button plc
Cover image: Buzz Pictures/Alamy
Illustrator: Bill Greenhead
Text design and typesetting: Nicholas Garner, Codesign
Educational consultants: Cliff Moon and Lorraine Petersen
Pictures: Alamy: pages 6, 10, 13, 22, 23, 24, 25, 33, 36,
37, 40, 42, 43; Buzz Pictures: pages 4, 5, 11, 16, 22, 23,
32, 33, 35, 41, 46; Getty Images: 8, 30, 34, 38, 39, 43.

This book should not
be used as a guide to
the sports shown in it.
The publishers accept
no responsibility for
any harm which might
result from taking
part in these sports.

British Library Cataloguing in Publication Data.
A CIP record for this book is available from the British
Library.

ISBN: 978-1-905056-91-0
Printed by Craftprint International Ltd, Singapore

Contents

Skydiving and parachuting

Are skydiving and parachuting the same thing?

No! But skydivers do both.

They put parachutes on their backs and go up in a plane. Then they jump out into free fall. This is called skydiving and it's lots of fun!

These people are skydiving.

Skydiving happens before
they open their parachutes.

These people are parachuting.

Parachutes

Parachutes used to be round.

Now, most parachutes are square.

Square parachutes are better than round parachutes.

They fly faster.

They turn faster.

They land better.

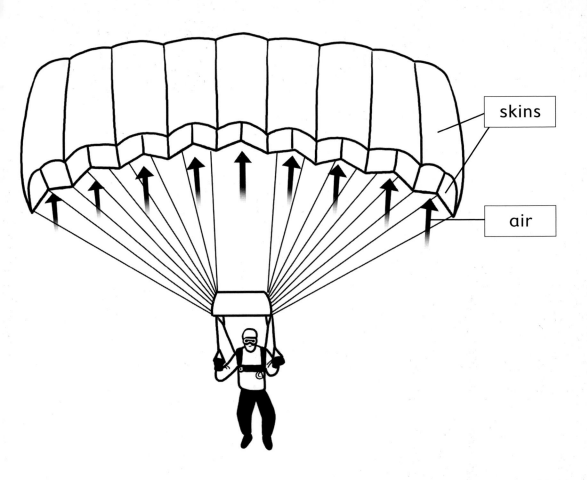

skins

air

Square parachutes have two layers called skins.

The skins fill with air when the parachute opens.

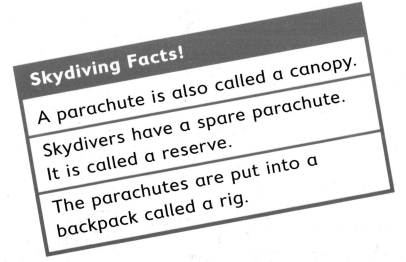

Skydiving Facts!

A parachute is also called a canopy.

Skydivers have a spare parachute.
It is called a reserve.

The parachutes are put into a
backpack called a rig.

Skydiving kit

Rig – holds parachute

Most skydivers wear a jumpsuit. The rig fits well over a jumpsuit.

Gloves – protect hands

This side lets you feel and grip.

Goggles – protect eyes

Skydiving Tips!

Make sure your goggles fit well.

Don't wear tinted goggles when you are learning!

Open face helmet – protects head

Skydiving Tips!

Make sure your helmet fits well.

You must wear goggles with an open face helmet.

Altimeter – gives altitude

You wear this altimeter on your hand. It shows you how high up you are.

Skydiving Tips!

You can also wear an altimeter in your helmet. It tells you how high up you are.

Get into skydiving

There are three ways to start skydiving.

Static line

A line pulls your
parachute out.

Skydiving course	Training
Static line	Six hours – one jump
AFF	Five days – ten jumps
Tandem	15 minutes – one jump

AFF

Two teachers jump with you.

The teachers communicate with hand signals.

Tandem

You are strapped to your teacher.

Cost	Is it for me?
Less than AFF or Tandem	Yes, if you want to try skydiving
More than Static line or Tandem	Yes, if you want to carry on skydiving
More than Static line and less than AFF	Yes, if you only want to do one jump

Money, money, money

Skydiving costs money.

What if you don't have any money?

Do it for charity!

Lots of charities will help you skydive for free.

You have to get **sponsorship** for the jump.

You can get skydiving gift vouchers.

They are better than socks!

Do it second-hand!

You can get your kit second-hand.

Warning!

Ask a good skydiver to check the kit first!

Skydivers for a Day
(Part one)

It started when Seb saw the ad.

WANT TO GO SKYDIVING?
WANT TO HELP A CHARITY?
YOU CAN DO BOTH!

"We've got to do this!" said Seb. "It's so easy. You get sponsorship. Then you go skydiving – for free."

I'm up for it – are you?

Great idea!

Cool!

We *said* we wanted to do it.

But what did we *think*?

We asked our parents.

Mark's mum said no.

"I'm not 16 yet," said Mark. "I can't do it."
"Bad luck!" said Seb.

Mark's mum works in a bank. The bank sponsored us £400.

Continued on page 20

Drop zones

You go skydiving at a drop zone.

People at the drop zone

Chief Instructor

Runs the centre.

Instructor

Teaches the skydivers.

Manifestor

Makes a list of skydivers for each **lift**.

The list is put on to a **manifest board**.

Drop Zone Controller

Runs the drop zone. Uses a **telemeter** to check that everything is OK.

Pilot

Flies the plane. The plane has to be in the right place at the right time.

Ground school

You go to **ground school** before you jump.

You learn lots of things there.

How to jump out of
the plane.

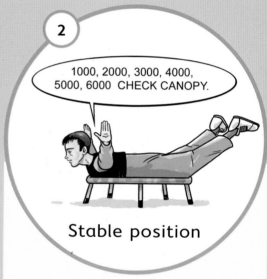

1000, 2000, 3000, 4000,
5000, 6000 CHECK CANOPY.

Stable position

What to do in free fall.

Troubleshooter
Problem
Your main parachute does not open
You land in a tree

How to fly the parachute.

How to land.
How to keep safe.

What do you do?

Cut away your main parachute.

Open your reserve parachute.

Do a **PLF** – a **Parachute Landing Fall.**

Skydivers for a Day
(Part two)

We still had to get £300. We asked the school to help.

The parents sponsored us £300 – now all we had to do was jump!

We went to **ground school** for a day.

The instructor showed us the kit.

He showed us how to jump out of the plane.

We learned what to do in free fall.

We learned how to fly the parachute – and how to land it.

Mark and his mum picked us up.

"How did it go?" asked Mark.

"Brilliantly!" said Seb. I didn't say anything.

Continued on page 26

The first jump

Flight line

Your kit is checked.

The instructor gives you a last talk.

The plane

You sit in your seat.

You do not move until you are told.

The exit

You go to the door.

You sit in the doorway.

You jump!

Skydiving

You get into the stable position.

You do the safety count.

Your parachute opens.

Landing

You head for the landing area.

You start to get lower.

You start to slow down.

You land!

First-time skydivers have a large landing area!

Using a parachute

How do I open the parachute?

Use the ripcord handle.

It is at the bottom of the parachute bag.

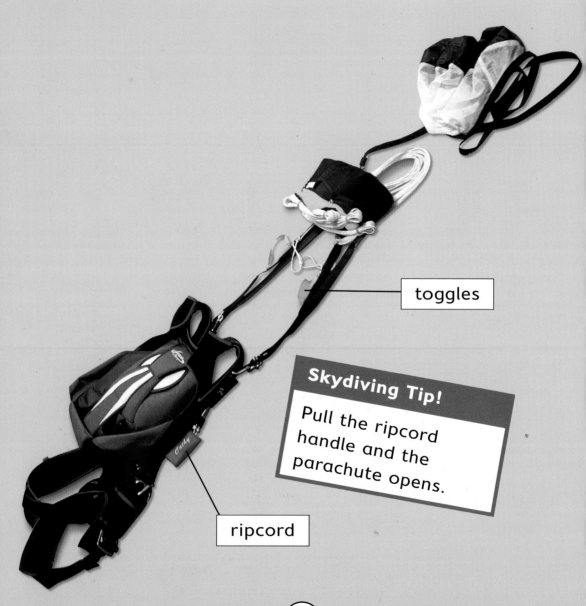

toggles

Skydiving Tip!

Pull the ripcord handle and the parachute opens.

ripcord

How do I fly the parachute?

Use the toggles — they are above your shoulders.

Skydiving Tips!

Pull one toggle to go right or left.

Pull both toggles to slow down.

How do I land the parachute?

Face into the wind.

Pull down both toggles.

Skydiving Tip!

Land with your knees bent.

Skydivers for a Day
(Part three)

I didn't sleep well that night. I had bad dreams about the jump.

Next morning, I called Seb ...

It was cold at the drop zone but the sky was clear. It was a good day for the jump.

We got ready. Then our kit was checked.
Our instructor went over everything one last
time, then he said "Good luck!".

We had to sit still in the plane.
Nobody moved.
Nobody spoke.

The same words went round in my head.
"I can't do this! I can't do this!"

Seb was first. He got ready to jump.

"Where is the drop zone?" he asked.
"It's in that huge field, you nut!" said the
instructor. "Don't worry. You can't miss it!"

I was the last to jump. My legs felt like jelly.
I sat down in the doorway.

Continued on the next page

Then I forgot to be scared. The only thing in my head was the training.

I jumped out ...

The wind rushed into my face. I was falling – fast!
Then there was a whoosh. My parachute opened.
I was flying!
I was as free as a bird.

Then I had to land. It was over too soon! Seb and Mark ran over to me.

"You were brilliant!" said Mark.

"I wasn't scared at all!" I shouted.

"Oh yes," said Seb. "And pigs can skydive!"

SKYDIVERS ON CLOUD NINE!

Rick and Seb did their parachute jump yesterday – and they still haven't come down to Earth!

What next?

I have done my first jump.
Can I skydive on my own?

No! You have to work up
to Category 8.

What jump did you do?	What can you do next?
Tandem jump	Do a static line jump OR Do an AFF course
Static line jump	Go to a Category System instructor – work up to Category 8 OR Do an AFF course
AFF course	Get to level 8 in the AFF course Do 10 more good jumps to get to Category 8!

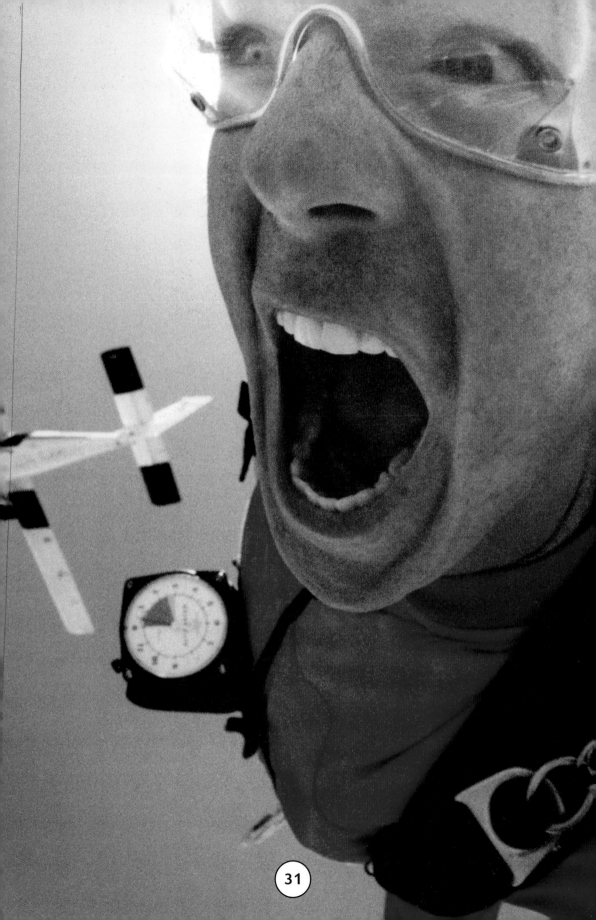

What happens when I get to Category 8?

You can skydive without an instructor.

You can learn a different kind of skydiving.

Free fall style

Freestyle

Skysurfing

Skydiving Facts!

There are competitions in free fall style, freestyle and skysurfing. You can also compete in:

- accuracy landing
- formation skydiving
- canopy formation
- freeflying

The classics

Accuracy landing and free fall style are called the **classics**.

Skydivers have been doing them for a long time.

Accuracy landing

What do you do?

Try to land on a 5 cm disc.

What happens in a competition?

An **AMD** shows how close each landing is.

The closest landing wins.

Free fall style

What do you do?

A set of turns and jumps in free fall.

A back loop

What happens in a competition?

Get the moves right and do them as fast as you can.

The fastest set of moves wins.

Formation skydiving

What is formation skydiving?

The skydivers make a pattern with their bodies.
The pattern is called a formation.

Formation Facts

You do the formation on the ground first. This is called a dirt dive.

What happens in a competition?

The skydivers do a set of formations.

They do the set as many times as they can.

Judges use videos to help them pick the best team.

Canopy formation

What is canopy formation?

Teams of skydivers make a pattern with their parachutes.

The pattern is called a formation.

What happens in a competition?

Competition	Rules
4-way rotations	Make a **stack** The skydiver on top comes down to the bottom Do this as many times as you can in $1\frac{1}{2}$ minutes
4-way sequential	Do a set of formations Do it as many times as you can in 2 minutes
8-way speed formation	Make a formation as fast as you can

More than 30 skydivers have made this formation.

Artistic events

There are three artistic events.
They are freestyle, skysurfing and freeflying.

Freestyle is doing acrobatics in the wind.

Skysurfers ride a board on the wind. They can go any way up.

Freeflyers do not use the stable position.

This is the Sit fly position.

This is the Head down position.

What happens in a competition?

A camera flyer takes a video and the judges watch it.

They give points for the skydiving and for the camera work.

BASE jumping

BASE jumping is **illegal** in the UK and many other countries. It is very dangerous.

BASE jumpers jump off objects. BASE stands for:

Buildings

Antennae

Spans

Earth

You have to jump from each of these things. Then you get a BASE number. A **camera flyer** makes a video.

Buildings

Antennae

The biggest **legal** BASE jump in the world is Bridge Day.

Bridge Day is held in America. The BASE jumping is only legal for six hours.

Spans

Earth

Quiz

1 What is another word for parachute?

2 What does an altimeter do?

3 What happens in a tandem parachute jump?

4 Your main parachute does not open. What two things should you do?

5 How do you slow down your parachute?

6 You get to Category 8. What two things can you do?

7 Skydivers try out formations on the ground. What is this called?

8 What is Canopy Formation?

9 Name two freeflying positions.

10 What does BASE stand for?

Glossary of terms

altitude	How high up you are from the ground or the sea.
AMD	Stands for Automatic Measuring Device – an electronic chip that shows how far away you land.
camera flyer	A skydiver who uses a camera to film jumps.
classics	A classic is something that has stood the test of time.
exit	The way out of a building, room or vehicle.
ground school	Training that happens on the ground.
illegal	Against the law.
legal	Not against the law.
lift	A group of skydivers jumping from one plane.
manifest board	A board that shows the skydivers jumping that day.
Parachute Landing Fall (PLF)	A way of rolling when you land – it protects your body.
stack	A canopy formation – the canopies go one on top of the other.
sponsorship	A person does a fund-raising event. He asks people to give him money for doing the event. The money is given to charity.
telemeter	A powerful pair of binoculars on a tripod – it also tells you how far away things are.

More resources

Books

The Skydiver's Handbook, Mike Turoff and Dan Poynter,
Publishers Group West (1-56860-087-9)
Everything you need in one book. There is also a CD ROM version –
Skydiving, A Multimedia Reference

Extreme Sports, Joe Tomlinson, Ed Leigh, Carlton Books Ltd
(1-84442-708-0)
Lots of information on skydiving and BASE jumping – lots of
photos, too.

Team Skydiving (Sports Alive), Charles and Linda George,
Capstone Press (0-73680-054-9)

Skydiving (Action Sports), Christopher Meeks, Capstone Press
(1-56065-051-6)

Magazines

Skydive – The Mag (The journal of the BPA)
You cannot buy this in the shops. You have to order it. You can also
read bits of the mag on a website:
http:/www.bpa.org.uk/skydive/frontpane.html
Lots of info and great photos.

Websites

http://www.bpa.org.uk
The official website of the British Parachuting Organisation. Info on
how to make your first jump – and what to do next!

http://www.jojaffa.com/guides/skydiving.htm
A clear and fun site about skydiving.

DVDs

Free fall Extreme – The Ultimate Skydiving Adventure (2001)
(Cat. No. B00005BJXD)
Feel as if you are up there with the skydivers!

Answers

1 Canopy.

2 It tells you your altitude.

3 You are strapped to your teacher.

4 Cut away your main parachute. Open your reserve parachute.

5 Pull both toggles.

6 You can skydive without a teacher. You can learn a different kind of skydiving.

7 A dirt dive.

8 Teams of skydivers make a pattern with their parachutes.

9 Sit fly and Head down.

10 Buildings, Antennae, Spans, Earth.

Index